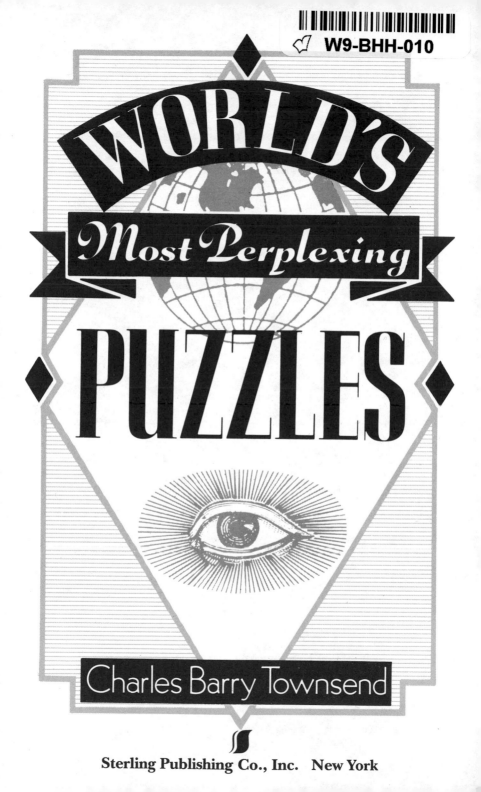

WORLD'S

Most Perplexing

PUZZLES

Charles Barry Townsend

Sterling Publishing Co., Inc.   New York

This book is dedicated to our son Chris to mark his halfway point through college. We're all mighty proud of the hard work you've done so far.

Library of Congress Cataloging-in-Publication Data

Townsend, Charles Barry.
   World's most perplexing puzzles   /   by Charles Barry Townsend.
      p.   cm.
   Includes index.
   ISBN 0-8069-1266-9
   1. Puzzles—Juvenile literature.   I. Title.
GV1493.T6878   1995
793.73—dc20
                                                     94-38522
                                                       CIP
                                                        AC

10   9   8   7   6   5   4   3   2

First paperback edition published in 1996 by
Sterling Publishing Company, Inc.
387 Park Avenue South, New York, N.Y. 10016
© 1995 by Charles Barry Townsend
Distributed in Canada by Sterling Publishing
% Canadian Manda Group, One Atlantic Avenue, Suite 105
Toronto, Ontario, Canada M6K 3E7
Distributed in Great Britain and Europe by Cassell PLC
Wellington House, 125 Strand, London WC2R 0BB, England
Distributed in Australia by Capricorn Link (Australia) Pty Ltd.
P.O. Box 6651, Baulkham Hills, Business Centre, NSW 2153, Australia
Manufactured in the United States of America
All rights reserved

Sterling ISBN 0-8069-1266-9 Trade
            0-8069-1267-7 Paper

Contents

INTRODUCTION

It's been a year since we sat down to a battle of wits. Six months ago I presented you with a new magic book, *World's Greatest Magic Tricks.* I hope you've had a chance to master some of its subtle mysteries. Now it's time to get back to some serious puzzling with this, my ninth book in a series devoted to bringing you the finest problems that have challenged thinking people for the past one hundred years.

Here are ninety-four problems. They deal with everything from heaven to hell and in between (you'll find a devil of a trick on page 6 and a heavenly inspiration from the Reverend I.N.Spire on page 23). Some other puzzling subjects that are touched on deal with a window cleaning company, a sunken treasure chest, a spaceship, a monkey who can paint portraits, some wagers that can win you a fortune, and a magic-square puzzle from your favorite substitute teacher, Ms. Priscilla Sunshine. You'll also get a full portion of riddles, some tricky poetic problems, and even a bang-up baffler employing fireworks.

And you'll find some problems using cards, checkers, watches, toothpicks, and insects. Stop by an archaeological dig, learn how best to juggle an egg on a plate, and try your luck at a close horse race.

Variety is always an aim in this series. That and a rich helping of amusing illustrations to enliven the proceedings. So, settle back and enter a world filled with many hours of pleasant puzzle solving.

CHARLES BARRY TOWNSEND

PUZZLES

World's Most Perplexing "Curtailing" Puzzles

> "Step right up, folks! We're going to play a little word game called 'Curtailing'! To play this game, chop off the last letter of a word in order to form another word. For example, to curtail a word meaning lamentation and leave a word meaning lament you would start with the word 'complaint.' Now, try to find the seven words called for below. If you get them all right, I'll give you a new car. However, if you miss any you'll have to forfeit something that we'll talk about later."

1) Curtail some stones and leave a hole.
2) Curtail a protection and leave a protection.
3) Curtail covered state and leave a covering.
4) Curtail to blemish and leave to blemish.
5) Curtail an intruder and leave a revenue.
6) Curtail to conceal and leave concealed.
7) Curtail a color and leave a fastener.

World's Most Perplexing "Math Signs" Puzzle

1234567889

"Put them on the desk, Bill. The answer must be in one of those books!"

Farleigh is at his wit's end trying to solve this old chestnut: Write down the digits 1 through 9 in the order shown above. Insert two minus signs and one plus sign between certain of the digits so that the result will be a mathematical expression equal to 100.

World's Most Perplexing "Bolt" Puzzle

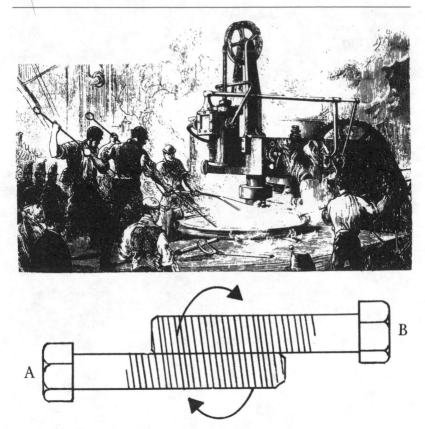

Down at the Burlington Bolts and Nuts factory no apprentice becomes a full-fledged foundryman without correctly answering the famous Bolt Puzzle! Each apprentice must take two large bolts that are exactly alike and place them together so the threads mesh, as shown below. The apprentice must then move bolt A around the bolt B, as indicated by the arrows, holding the bolts tightly so they do not rotate while this is being done. The question to be answered is: Will the heads of the bolts move closer together, move farther apart, or remain the same distance from one another?

World's Most Perplexing "Cleaning" Puzzle

WINDOW CLEANING

The Checkerboard Square Window Cleaning Company landed a big contract to clean the windows and mirrors at the Little Versailles Clothing Emporium. However, in estimating the job the foreman came up with the following problem: if two men could clean 60 windows in 7 hours and 20 minutes how long would it take one man to clean the 30 mirrors throughout the building. All the windows and mirrors are rectangular and they are all the same size. You have 30 seconds to squeak out the answer.

World's Most Perplexing "Tin Man" Puzzle

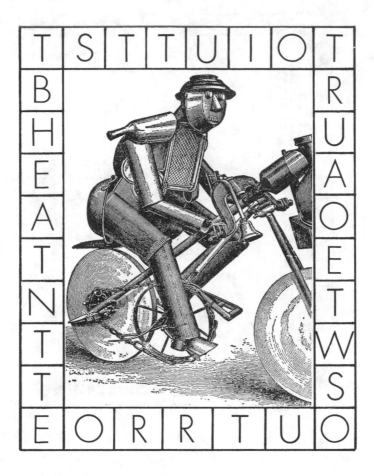

Pictured above is that symbol of early American salesmanship, the tin man. The motto of this industrious merchandiser is hidden in the above frame of letters. To find it, start at any letter and go around the frame twice, reading every other letter as you go. This could also be the motto of America's senior citizens.

World's Most Perplexing "Hidden Towns" Puzzle

HOW WE KNEW

How Anna polishes the silver when Jack is expected.

BECALMED

Such little puffs of air have no effect on the yachts.

Here we have two delightful puzzles from the pen of America's greatest puzzler, Sam Loyd. Hidden in the description under each picture is the locality of the incident depicted. You have one minute to find each town.

World's Most Perplexing "Treasure" Puzzle

In 1639 an English ship returning from a trip to the Holy Land sank off the coast of North Africa. Among the items lost was a treasure chest belonging to the bishop of Bristol. This chest could only by opened by setting the three dials on its side to positions that would spell out a three-letter English word appropriate to its owner. See if you can decipher the lock's secret before the octopus dispatches yonder diver and turns his attentions to you!

World's Most Perplexing "Chocolate" Puzzle

"Look at this huge piece of chocolate, Mama! Papa says we can have some just as soon as we solve his famous 'Squares of Salzburg' candy puzzle!"

In the Squares of Salzburg puzzle the problem is to take a giant slab of chocolate made up of twenty two-inch squares, and to cut it into nine pieces that can then be rearranged to form four perfect squares all exactly the same size. I have a feeling that this puzzle will disappear long before it is solved.

World's Most Perplexing " Spaceship" Puzzle

The latest sensation to come out of Europe is the discovery of an alien spaceship locked in an ice cave in northern Sweden. The ship and its crew have been perfectly preserved. Judging by the above photo, it seems that the aliens also used a numbering system similar to ours. A puzzle enthusiast at NASA noted that if you were to rearrange the ten numbers in the ship's identification decal the sum of the four numbers that make up each of the four large triangles would be equal to 50 (upper left, upper right, lower center, and upside-down center). Is he right?

World's Most Perplexing "Lightning Calculator" Puzzle

24	11	3	20	7	24	11	3	20	7
5	17	9	21	13	5	17	9	21	13
6	23	15	2	19	6	23	15	2	19
12	4	16	8	25	12	4	16	8	25
18	10	22	14	1	18	10	22	14	1
24	11	3	20	7	24	11	3	20	7
5	17	9	21	13	5	17	9	21	13
6	23	15	2	19	6	23	15	2	19
12	4	16	8	25	12	4	16	8	25
18	10	22	14	1	18	10	22	14	1

When you have mastered this puzzle you will be able to bill yourself as "The Lightning Calculator." Place a copy of the above grid on the table along with a 2-inch piece of a plastic coffee stirrer. Have someone place it on the grid so it covers any six numbers horizontally or vertically. You then instantly tell the person what the sum is of the six numbers so covered. Repeat this several times and then finally turn your back and tell the person to place the stirrer diagonally on the grid so that it covers five numbers. You immediately announce the sum without turning around. See if you can discern the secret of this mystery before turning to the answers section.

World's Most Perplexing "Animal" Puzzle

"Let's have a game of 'collective animal nouns' while we're waiting for Pigeon and Dove to arrive!"

"You mean like a 'litter of pups,' or a 'pride of lions'?"

"Exactly, Beakie! Shall we say a dollar a noun?"

It's Saturday night at the Pigeon Côte Club and the betting gentry are hot to trot. How many of the following "collective nouns" would you win a dollar on?

1) A doylt of _____.
2) A gaggle of _____.
3) A rout of _____.
4) A troop of _____.
5) A leap of _____.
6) A skulk of _____.
7) A sloth of _____.
8) A muster of _____.

World's Most Perplexing "Match" Puzzle

Edgar Puffington's pipe is so foul-smelling, his boss makes him work in the shipping bay. Edgar gets even by winning large matchstick bets with his boss every payday. Last week he challenged his boss with the 24 matches arranged as shown above. The pattern forms nine squares. The puzzle is to remove eight of these matches in such a way as to leave three squares.

World's Most Perplexing "Domino" Puzzle

Domino problems were the theme of last week's Puzzle Club Dinner and Dance. Here's the winning stumper: Take the 28 dominos in a set and form seven squares using 4 dominos per square. The sum of the pips on each side of any square must be the same. Here's the first one; it's up to you to find the rest.

World's Most Perplexing "Line" Puzzle

"Ladies and gentlemen, we are happy to present Jocko, the simian Shakespearean sketcher and portrait painter extraordinaire! His drawings of the Bard sell for hundreds of bananas each. The amazing Jocko drew the above puzzle portrait using one continuous line. At no point does the line cross over itself. Can you duplicate this amazing artistic feat?"

World's Most Perplexing "Card" Puzzle

"*My name is John Henry Anderson, better known as 'The Wizard of the North.' During the intermission I would like to show you an interesting betting proposition. In full view of your audience arrange a deck of cards so every other card from the top down alternates in color: black, red, black, red, etc. Once this is done, cut the deck in two and thoroughly riffle-shuffle the cards together. Now, square up the deck and state that you will turn the cards over two at a time going through the entire deck. For every pair of the same color you will pay two dollars, and for every pair that has a black and a red card you expect to be paid one dollar.*

"*How can you be sure of always winning such a wager?*"

World's Most Perplexing "Hidden Face" Puzzle

BOARDERS TAKEN IN

The farmer has a little tin,
Which he has saved with care;
All summer he took boarders in
And now takes in the fair.

FIND A SUMMER BOARDER

Picture puzzles were quite popular back at the turn of the century. Here's an interesting one that appeared in 1909. Close inspection will reveal the face of Hiram's star summer boarder. You are allowed no more than 60 seconds to find this shy gentleman.

World's Most Perplexing "Magic Square" Puzzle

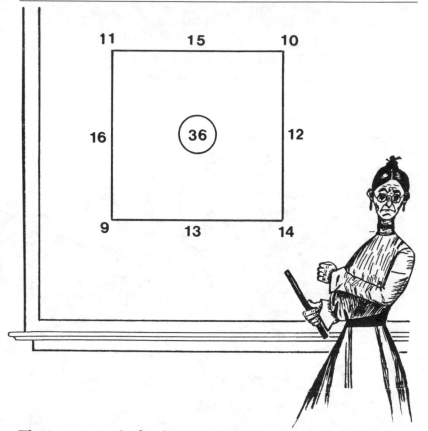

That nonpareil of substitute teachers, Ms. Priscilla Sunshine, will conduct today's math class. Listen up!

"Your regular teacher, Mr. Tracy, informs me that you need some extra practice in solving magic squares. On the blackboard I've arranged the numbers 9 through 16 around the sides of a square in such a manner that the sum of the three numbers on any one side is 36. Your problem is to rearrange these eight numbers so that the sum of the three numbers on any one side will be 37.

"While you're solving that one, I'll put some more up on the other board!"

World's Most Perplexing "Cross" Puzzle

"Of course, 'P.I.P.' stands for 'Puzzle In Peace.' And the rest of the inscription reads:

'Rend the cross above our hearts,
Into four identical stony parts.
Bring all back together with great care,
To form a cross within a square!'"

The Reverend I.N. Spire has stumbled across the resting place of a puzzling couple. Can you cut the above cross into four identical pieces and then reassemble them into a square that contains a cross?

World's Most Perplexing "What, When, and Why" Puzzles

> "What makes an empty match box superior to any other?"
>
> "When is a wall like a fish?"
>
> "Why did Babe Ruth make so much money?"
>
> "What is the difference between a mountain and a pill?"
>
> "When is a window like a star?"
>
> "Why is a hen sitting on a fence like a penny?"
>
> "What state is round at both ends and tall in the middle?"

The Sawmill Valley "What, When, and Why Septet" is shown here warming up for their turn at the annual Northwest Riddle Contest at the Sourdough County Fair back in 1903. How many of these melodic mysteries can you decipher?

World's Most Perplexing "Betting" Puzzle

"Watching those two reminds me of a cardsharp I met out in the gold fields. He'd take the top 20 cards from a deck, turn them face-up and shuffle them into the rest of the deck. Then he'd hand you the deck and invite you to shuffle it as many times as you liked until you were satisfied that the face-up cards were well mixed in. He then had you take off the top 20 cards and hand them to him under the table. A few seconds later he brought them out and placed them on the table declaring that there were now as many face-up cards in his stack as there were in the remaining 32 cards in your stack. I never knew him to miss. He made more money with that trick than I did panning gold!"

Can you figure out how Faro Farley was able to rearrange the cards under the table without seeing them?

World's Most Perplexing "Fireworks" Puzzle

No. 6416. Laughing Uncle.
When lit, goes off with a bang, throwing out a large quantity of entertaining parlor jokes.
Each ....10 cents

Tower of Gold. 5cents When lit, it goes off with a loud bang, throwing out a large quantity miniature gold and silver coins,

No. 6327 E. Joke Bottle Corks.
Each....................................1 cent

Comical Nut Cracker. .... 25 cent
Throws out jokes, riddles, etc.,

At the turn of the century Grandpa Townsend liked to celebrate a birthday with what was then thought to be harmless indoor fireworks. For one party he spent $2.42 for a variety of items. He bought the same number of 1¢ and 5¢ items. Also, the total sums spent on the 10¢ and 25¢ items were both the same. Can you figure out how many of each type were purchased and how much was spent on each type?

World's Most Perplexing "Archaeology" Puzzle

"Well, Petrie, what do you make of this Greek painting? When our men cleaned the grime and dirt from this wall we found this amazing picture of Bacchus, god of wine!"

"I agree, Hawkings, your find is quite amazing. However, I think it's a fake. There's something strange about the picture. The more I look at it, the more confusing it becomes."

It's interesting Petrie finds this portrait a bit intoxicating. Can you focus in on the problem?

World's Most Perplexing "Aces and Kings" Puzzle

"Alakazam, let the other cards scram! Your card, madame, is . . . the five of clubs!

"And now for an amusing card puzzle I call 'Aces and Kings.' Here, sir, are the four aces and four kings from a deck of cards. I challenge you to arrange them in such an order that when you alternately deal them face-up onto the table they will be in the order king, ace, king, ace, king, ace and king, ace. The deal must go as follows: Hold the pack of eight cards face-down. Transfer the top card to the bottom of the pack and turn the next card over and place it face-up on the the table. Continue in this manner until all eight cards are on the table.

"If you solve this problem by the end of my act you'll get to assist me in the sensational 'French Guillotine Mystery.' "

Ned "King of Kards" Fairbanks has provided our readers with an interesting challenge. Let's see if you can discover the secret before the blade falls.

World's Most Perplexing "Juggling" Puzzle

"To make an egg dance on the bottom of a plate, first boil it hard; then set it on its large end in the center of the plate, and, holding the latter horizontal, give it a rotation in a horizontal plane; the egg will keep spinning like a top. With practice, the egg may be made to assume the vertical position after being laid on its side. To facilitate prompt obedience on the part of the egg, hold it vertical, with the large end downward, while it is being boiled. To make the trick still more easy to perform, lay the plate on a table with the edge projecting beyond that of the table, and then start the egg spinning by use of the thumb and fingers. The projecting position of the plate will enable you to grasp this latter quickly with the right hand, and then all that you will have to do will be to keep the egg spinning by giving the plate its rotating motion." (Magazine article, circa 1900.)

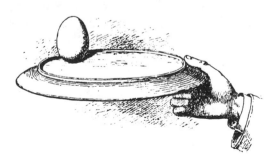

World's Most Perplexing "Book" Puzzle

First Scholar: "It clearly states in the unabridged edition of Henri Decremps' *La Magie Blanche Dévoilée* (Natural Magic Disclosed) that it is possible to concentrate your breath to such a degree that you can actually knock fairly heavy objects over with it. As an example he tells of how the magician Pinetti placed a large book on top of a massive dictionary and then proceeded to topple both with a few puffs of his breath."

Second Scholar: "There has to be more to it than that. Perhaps he used a plate lifter!"

Can the reader help these two savants out by discovering the secret to this well-kept mystery?

World's Most Perplexing "Checker" Puzzle

Pop Bentley's perfect record against Cy Corncrib is still intact. Pop just beat Cy for the umpteenth time with one of his patented slam-bang endings. Pop was playing the black pieces and it was his turn. The white pieces were moving up the board, while the black were moving down. What series of moves did Pop use to dispatch Cy so quickly?

World's Most Perplexing "Toothpick" Puzzle

World's Most Perplexing "Cardboard" Puzzle

Carlton, the Cardboard Conjurer Extraordinaire, is seen here performing his famous "Square Within a Square" magic puzzle. First he takes a two-foot square of cardboard with one corner cut out and places it on a sheet of glass. Slowly it rises into the air, where it hangs suspended about a foot above the glass. Next, the cardboard splits itself into two pieces which then revolve around each other until they finally come back together in the form of a perfect two-foot square with a one-foot-square hole in the center. The cardboard is then passed around for examination, and Carlton takes his bow.

How would you cut the cardboard to effect this miracle?

World's Most Perplexing "Sandwich" Puzzle

"My dear Camilla, haven't you finished making those sandwiches yet? How many have you made? The last foursome is approaching the eighteenth green now. My reputation as host for this tournament is on the line!"

"Oh, keep your shirt on, Norbert. If you had helped me with the asparagus sandwiches I'd have been finished an hour ago. If you really want to know how many sandwiches are made I'll give you a hint. If you divide the total number of sandwiches by 2, 3, 4, 5, or 6 you would find that you always have a remainder. However, if you divide the total by 11 you will get no remainder. What you are looking for is the smallest total that will satisfy these conditions. Now here they come. Start pouring the sarsaparilla."

World's Most Perplexing "Rebus" Puzzle

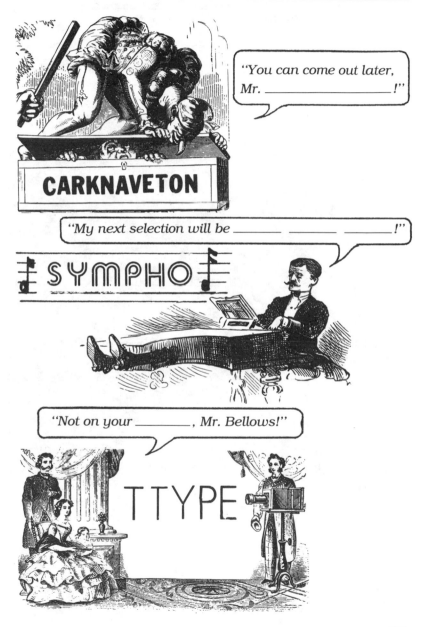

World's Most Perplexing "Racing" Puzzle

Atlantic City—Sixth Race						
Horses	1	2	3	4	5	Fin
Eight Ball	6	2	3	5	4	1
Hay Burner	3	6	1	4	5	2
Slow Start	5	1	6	2	4	3
No Luck	5	6	1	2	3	4
Swayback	4	1	3	6	2	5
Last In	2	5	3	1	4	6

LAYING WAGERS ON THE RACES AT THE OCEAN HOTEL

It's the summer of 1903 and the high-rollers are busy deciding which horses to bet on for the next race. In the sixth race six horses competed in a six-furlong affair that ended as shown on the above tote board. One improver of the breed, an inveterate puzzler, noted that an interesting puzzle would be to rearrange the positions of the horses in the above columns so the numbers 1 through 6 would appear only once in every row and column, making a neat numeric magic square. What are the odds you can solve it in ten minutes flat?

World's Most Perplexing "Synonym" Puzzle

"Quick, driver, to the main branch of the public library, and don't spare the whip! I'm late for the annual New York City Synonym Contest!"

We're happy to report that the above gentleman made it to the contest on time and won first prize in the "Five-Letter Word" contest. He had to find a five-letter synonym beginning with the letter "Q" for each of the following words:

1) cover
2) doubt
3) entirely
4) fraud
5) game bird
6) line
7) measure
8) monarch
9) nimble
10) particle
11) pen
12) scruple
13) search
14) secluded
15) share
16) subdue
17) suppress
18) swallow
19) tremble
20) whip

World's Most Perplexing "Age" Puzzle

"Farewell, Bartlett, you bum! I knew you had a roving eye, but I never thought you'd toss me aside for a woman you think is younger than I. And to think you had the nerve to ask me my age just to make sure I'm older. Well, I'll tell you, all right, but in my own way. If you have anything between those oversized ears of yours, you just might be able to figure this out: My age today is thrice what my age will be three years from now minus thrice what my age was three years ago!"

It sounds as if Heloise is well rid of her not-so-faithful swain, Bartlett. She has a rather neat way, though, of divulging her age. Is she older than she looks, or is Bartlett letting Ms. Right slip through his fingers?

World's Most Perplexing "Grand Prize" Puzzle

Problem No. 99

$$\underline{12 \qquad 6}$$
$$345 \quad 789$$

"Look, chums," crowed Winthrop Swellhead, "a Waterbury watch! I won this for solving problem 99. The numbers 1 through 9 were placed above or below a line according to some scheme. I had to determine where the next number, 10, was to go. The answer was mere child's play!"

World's Most Perplexing "Watch" Puzzle

The Clancy brothers were the crackerjack clean-up crew in the old Flatiron Building in New York City. In appreciation for their punctuality the owners gave each of them a Callander watch. Then the trouble began. While Brian's watch kept perfect time, Barry's lost a minute a day and Patrick's gained a minute a day. If the fellows set their watches to the correct time at noon the day they received them and never reset them after that, how many days would pass before the three watches would again all show the correct time at noon?

World's Most Perplexing "Checking" Puzzle

"Here's a puzzle to exercise your 'little grey cells' with. Last night I dropped into a rather nice watering hole. I don't remember which one, but when it came time to leave I discovered I was all out of ready cash. Luckily, I did have a personal check from old Mr. Sommes and I asked the bartender if he would cash it. He was a good chap and said he would be delighted to. However, he mistakenly gave me in dollars what he should have given me in cents and in cents what he should have given me in dollars. I then paid my bar tab, which was $4.45, and went home. When I counted my money, I discovered I had twice as much as the original check was made out for.

"And now for the puzzle. Can you tell me what amount the check was originally made out for?"

"You solved my problem concerning last night's short register, Mr. Bender. You were here last night and I cashed your check. I'll add the difference to your bar tab now!"

World's Most Perplexing "Rearranging" Puzzle

TCLTUACA
RZIBRTIA
OULHNULO

TENAWCOP
YVRIKEKAJ
GESPRIANO

ORNONAG
SSRFACONCAIN
NKGNGHOO

TRHMUPTOOS
LENUMEOBR
BNACSAALAC

The U.S.S. *Extravagantic* celebrated its maiden voyage in 1922 by taking a three-month cruise around the world. The lucky passengers visited dozens of famous cities along the way. We've scrambled the names of twelve of them to give you the opportunity to join in the fun. Let's see if you can unscramble them before it's time to disembark.

World's Most Perplexing "Millennium" Puzzle

X	X	507	X
506	X	X	X
X	509	X	X
X	X	X	508

Although the second millennium is still several years away we would like to be among the first to start the celebrating with a special "Millennium Magic Square" puzzle. We've set up a magic square that's designed to total 2000 in any direction, horizontally, vertically, and diagonally corner to corner. We've entered four of the numbers for you. The remaining twelve three-digit numbers, 492 through 503, inclusive, are for you to enter. You have until January 1, 2000, to finish the square.

World's Most Perplexing "Ancient" Puzzle

"Before taking up the matter of point-shaving in the last Olympic Games, let's break the tension with a puzzle I heard in the agora yesterday. I met the Roman, Gaius Perplexus, and he told me he had been exiled to Athens for stumping the emperor with the following problem:
  'One third of twelve if you divide,
      By just one fifth of seven,
    The true result (it has been tried)
      Exactly is eleven.'
  "I'll give an amphora of wine to the first citizen who can solve it!"

World's Most Perplexing "Insect" Puzzle

When things slow down in the winter, the folks in Bugville pass the time of day solving "Insect Spelling Bee's." The one they're working on now requires the player to use the sixteen letters on the billboard to spell the names of eight different insects. Each letter can only be used once in a name. Don't get stung winging this one!

World's Most Perplexing "Electricity" Puzzle

During the early days of electricity Mr. Jenkins was one of a number of daring entertainers who demonstrated this phenomenon to the public. One of his most interesting items was a "paper motor." He would take a four-inch square of stiff paper, bend two opposite corners, as shown above, find the center of the card, and balance it upon the point of a needle that had been stuck upright in a cork. Mr. Jenkins, who claimed that his body was always highly charged with electricity, would then bring his hands up close to the card, which would then start to spin madly on the point of the pin. Try discovering Mr. Jenkins's secret before looking in the answer section of this book.

World's Most Perplexing "Triangle" Puzzle

"Rosalinde, where in the world did that strange ornament on top of yonder tower come from?"

"Why, Sir Guy of Grimsby brought it back from the Crusades. The design is made by welding eighteen rods together forming nine triangles. There's a puzzle associated with it. It's possible to remove three of the rods and be left with seven triangles. If you can figure it out I'll let you wear my handkerchief in the joust tomorrow."

Can you help the young man out?

World's Most Perplexing "Change-the-Word" Puzzle

Change-The-Word Puzzles

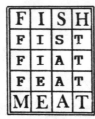

M	O	R	E
L	O	R	E
L	O	S	E
L	O	S	S
L	E	S	S

F	I	S	H
F	I	S	T
F	I	A	T
F	E	A	T
M	E	A	T

W	A	R	M
W	A	R	D
W	O	R	D
C	O	R	D
C	O	L	D

"In Change-the-Word puzzles you are required to change the top word into the bottom word by changing one letter at a time as you go down the ladder. Each change must produce a new word. Try the following:

1) BOAT to CASH   2) STAR to FEET   3) ROAD to COIL
4) BELL to SIFT   5) CALL to MUTE   6) RAFT to WING

On his way to Saint Elmo's Prep, young Tom enjoys passing the time with a few puzzles as a way of sharpening his wits for Professor Grill's math class.

World's Most Perplexing "Dog House" Puzzle

Our dog Jackie is pictured here showing off her new house to her friends. For our puzzle we've outlined the house using ten matchsticks. Her friends like it all right but think it should be turned 90 degrees so it faces the road. Can you accomplish this by moving two of the matches to new positions?

World's Most Perplexing "Sherlock Holmes" Puzzle

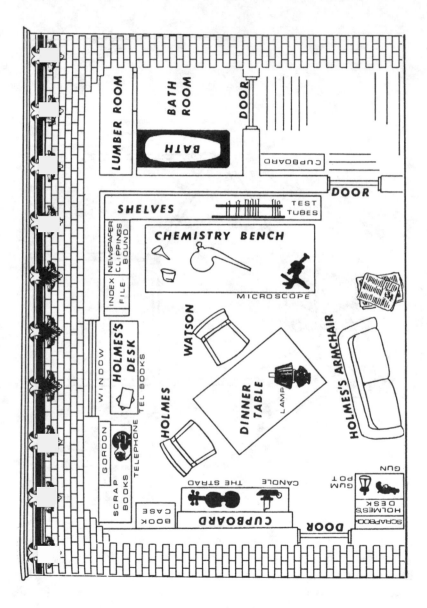

World's Most Perplexing "Sherlock Holmes" Puzzle

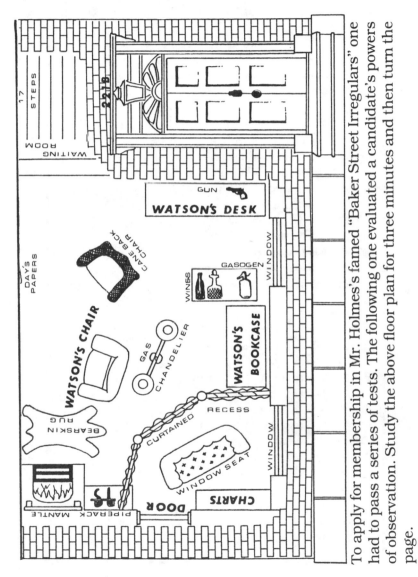

To apply for membership in Mr. Holmes's famed "Baker Street Irregulars" one had to pass a series of tests. The following one evaluated a candidate's powers of observation. Study the above floor plan for three minutes and then turn the page.

World's Most Perplexing "Sherlock Holmes" Puzzle

THE SHERLOCK HOLMES OBSERVATIONAL TEST

1) Where is Holmes's gun? Watson's gun?
2) Where is the lumber room?
3) Draw in Holmes's armchair.
4) Where is the Stradivarius?
5) Draw in the window seat.
6) What is on the dinner table?
7) Where is the microscope?
8) Where is the telephone?
9) Where is the index file?
10) Where are the day's papers?
11) Where is the gasogen?
12) Where is the cupboard?
13) How many steps are there up to Holmes's door?
14) Where is the piperack?
15) Where are the charts kept?
16) Where is Watson's desk?
17) Where is the gum pot?
18) Draw in Watson's chair.
19) Where are the scrapbooks? (two places)
20) Where is the candle?
21) Where is the bookcase?
22) Where are the wine bottles?
23) Draw in the gas chandelier.
24) Where are the test tubes?
25) What is on the floor in front of the fireplace?
26) Where are the telephone books?
27) Where is Watson's bookcase?
28) Where is Holmes's dinner table chair?
29) Draw in the caneback chair.
30) Where are the bound newspaper clippings?
31) Where is General Gordon's picture hung?
32) Where is the chemistry bench?

World's Most Perplexing "Sherlock Holmes" Puzzle

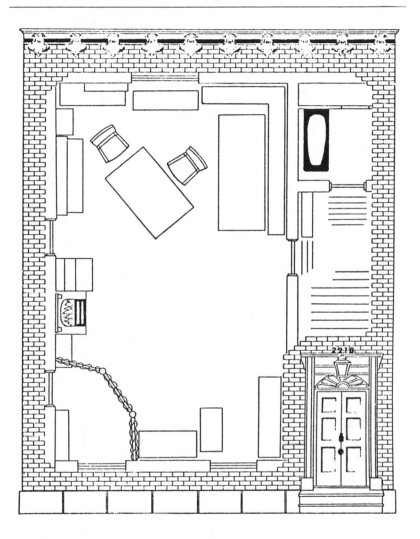

On the opposite page you will find the 32 questions that make up the "Sherlock Holmes Observational Test." If you answer at least 25 correctly you qualify as a junior member. The above layout should help you in locating the objects called for.

World's Most Perplexing "Chickenman" Puzzle

"My head and tail both equal are,
   My middle slender as a bee.
Whether I stand on head or heel
   Is quite the same to you or me.
But if my head should be cut off,
   The matter's true, though passing strange
Directly I to nothing change."

Challenging the reader to a battle of wits is the dreaded Chickenman. Free at last from the Tree of 10,000 Thorns, he's lean and mean and mighty hungry. Industrial pollution caused the thorns to fall off the tree and now Chickenman is looking for his first square meal in 700 years. Answer his poetic question and he'll pass you by. Fail and it's pass-the-seasoning time.

World's Most Perplexing "Barber" Puzzle

"So this barber-shop-supply salesman comes by yesterday and tries to sell me a pair of Never-Need-Sharpening scissors for $9.00 a pair. 'What are they made of, gold?' I sez! 'How much do you make on such a sale?'

" 'Well, sir,' he sez to me, 'I'll tell you what I'll do. I'll sell you two pairs of scissors for only $15.00. And believe it or not, I'll still only be making the same commission I would selling one pair!'

" 'All right,' I sez, 'I'll buy two pairs if you'll throw in six bottles of Tiger Lily cologne.' "

"Sounds like a good deal, Meldon. Not counting the cologne, how much commission do you think the dude earned?"

Answer this one and you're next in the chair!

World's Most Perplexing "Christmas" Puzzle

Christmas in the good old days! Mother around the tree with her children. Father snoozing in his favorite chair. This is a special day for three of their children because they were also born on Christmas Day. Let's see if you can figure out their ages. Today Barton is as old as the combined ages of Wendel and Susan. Last Christmas Wendel was twice as old as Susan. Finally, two years from now, Barton will be twice as old as Susan.

Can you dope out their ages before the turkey and fixings are brought to the table?

World's Most Perplexing "Number" Puzzle

$$\begin{array}{r} ABCDE \\ \times 4 \\ \hline EDCBA \end{array}$$

The students have painted a new wall-art puzzle on the building across from Professor Flunkum's office, and he has missed his morning classes trying to figure it out. To solve it you have to substitute any of the digits 0 through 9 for the letters to create a correct arithmetical expression. The same digit must be used for the same letter. The professor looks as though he's finished for the day.

World's Most Perplexing "Archery" Puzzle

Back at the turn of the century the Hood sisters were an unbeatable combination when it came to team competition in competitive archery. After having been beaten once too often by the ladies, ex-champion Hayward Nottingham challenged them to unravel an archery puzzle that he secretly considered unsolvable. Each sister had to shoot three arrows into the target. The value of the six hits had to total 21. When the judges added up their hits they announced that the sisters had failed the challenge.

"Not so fast," said Roberta Hood. "If you add them up again I think you'll find that we have won!"

She was right. How did the sisters win the bet?

World's Most Perplexing "Magic Kettle" Puzzle

"A farmer brought two cages of animals to market. One contained rabbits and the other contained pheasants. When asked how many of each he had, the farmer replied:

'The total number of animals in these two cages have thirty-five heads and ninety-four feet. Knowing that, you should be able to answer your own question!'"

Pictured here is that famous Victorian entertainer, Puzzling Prendergast, the prince of parlor prestidigitators, and his talking tea kettle. It has never been determined just how Prendergast made the kettle talk, but ventriloquism has been hinted at. However, his problems were always first rate. Can you solve the above potted problem?

World's Most Perplexing "Santa" Puzzle

Here's an excellent puzzle for your next Christmas party. In the above square we have two pictures of Santa Claus. Run off a dozen copies of the square and hand them out to your guests. Tell them that in order to solve the Santa puzzle they must first cut the square into four parts and then reassemble the pieces into two separate squares, each square containing one complete Santa. A candy cane to the first one who solves it!

World's Most Perplexing "Pentagram" Puzzle

This early nineteenth-century performer certainly had a colorful act. However, it seems his rather thin assistant had doubts concerning his abilities. In the Star of Pythagoras, pictured above, the puzzler must rearrange the ten numbers in the circles so the four numbers along any of the five lines of the pentagram will add up to 24. How would you do it?

World's Most Perplexing "Blacksmith" Puzzle

Cactus Jack, the cook out at the Puzzle-R-Ranch, sent word into town that he needed a new dinner bell. The local blacksmith, "Biceps" O'Bryan, having somewhat of a whimsical way about him, hammered out an iron bell in the shape of the famous "Lone Star Line Puzzle" and sent it to Cactus the next day. For those of you who are new to this type of puzzle, the problem is to draw the star emblem using one continuous line that doesn't cross itself at any point or go back over any part already drawn.

World's Most Perplexing "Solid Shape" Puzzle

"Now students, pay attention. Before we study the supernatural powers of the Infinite Sided Solid of Fra Sebastian, let us review the surface properties of some simple shapes. Please give me the names of the solids that:

1) Have only one surface.
2) Have only two surfaces.
3) Have only three surfaces.
4) Have only four surfaces.
5) Have only five surfaces.
6) Have only six surfaces."

You have 60 seconds to complete this test.

World's Most Perplexing "Tailors" Puzzle

To celebrate their Spring Opening in 1892 the Jacobs Brothers were offering Clay's Diagonal suits for $12. The following puzzle concerns their work habits. There were two chairs and three stools in their shop. Can you figure out where each of them sat from the following facts?

Nathan and Saul used the same kind of seat.
Saul and David sat on different types of seats.
David and Ira sat on different types of seats.

World's Most Perplexing "Musical" Puzzle

It was opening night, and the Wunderkinder of Seattle, Washington, Olaf and Katrina Gustafsonn, were about to bring the house down when the last seven notes of their Concerto for Spotted Owl came out upside down. Can you save the day and turn the seven notes right side up in three moves? During each move you must turn any three notes upside down.

World's Most Perplexing "Doctor" Puzzle

"Now don't despair, Mrs. Wisteria. You only have a mild case of puzzletosis. Mind, now, if not properly treated this can lead to more serious complications. I suggest you cut back to one puzzle a day, and cryptograms are strictly forbidden. Now, let's see if together we can't solve your problem, so I can get back to St. Billum's Hospital. The puzzle that put you out of sorts stated you must prove that eleven plus two equals one! That's an easy problem, although I'll wager no army man could solve it!"

World's Most Perplexing "Color" Puzzle

"Oh, Ramon, what will happen to our careers when color comes to the movies?"

"Our pasty complexions will doom us to selected black-and-white short subjects, my dear!"

Ramon and Rita's fear of technical advancements brings to mind a colorful test. The following ten statements each define a word whose first few letters spell a color. Ten out of ten will earn you a screen test.

1) On the ocean. (*White*cap)
2) A first starter
3) Found in pies
4) Some find it tasty
5) A type of building
6) Lacking in sense
7) The ape man
8) Best in the shade
9) An unpleasant sight
10) A strong liquid

World's Most Perplexing "Reverse Word" Puzzle

Alice's magic mirror would be a great help in solving the following reverse-word puzzles. Each of the lines in the three couplets below defines a word. The word defined in the second line is the reverse in spelling but not meaning of the word defined in the first line.

1) This form of exercise is easy to do;
   Turn it around, and your best friends are
   with you.

2) If you get out of this, then things will get hot;
   Turn it around, and you'll rest on a cot.

3) On this day we dance until we're beat;
   Turn me around, and we'll dig up a treat.

World's Most Perplexing "Apple" Puzzle

"Farmer Sy Corncrib brought a basket of apples into his kitchen and had his six sons line up. The basket contained six apples. After he divided them equally among his sons one apple was left in the basket. He did not cut or smash up any of the apples. How did he do it?"

"Land 'o Goshen! What a persnickety problem! I'll be up until nine o'clock trying to solve this one!"

Given enough time and her Holloway Reading Stand, there wasn't any puzzle that Maude Marionberry couldn't solve. How do you think Sy did it?

World's Most Perplexing "Word Square" Puzzle

"That, my dear, is this year's winner in the 'Word Square' painting contest. To solve it you must use the same five words both horizontally and vertically. The answer is in the back of your program!"

The following hints concerning the definitions of the five words should help the reader solve this interesting little problem:

1) Filled
2) To make up
3) A salutation
4) Follow in order
5) To hinder

World's Most Perplexing "Poetry" Puzzle

"You may be rich in yachts and pearls,
  You may hang around with dukes and earls;
You may have your weight in silver and gold,
  But when it comes to marriage, you're too old!"

"I know, Philomena, I look a bit seasoned, but really, I'm still a young buck at heart:
  If to my age there added be,
    One half, one third, and three times three;
  Six score and ten the sum you'll see,
    Pray find out what my age may be!"

Oswald should have left well enough alone. Once Philomena deciphers his age from that bit of doggerel he'll be shown the door pronto. Can you figure out the ardent swain's age?

World's Most Perplexing "Sphinx" Puzzle

Looking back in history we find the world's first great puzzler, Stumpumost II. He has a brand-new problem titled "The Second Riddle of the Sphinx" to stump his courtiers with. The solver must divide the above minimalist drawing of a sphinx into four equal, identically shaped pieces. The pieces must also have the same shape as the original drawing of the Sphinx. Let's see if you can dig up the answer.

World's Most Perplexing "Castle" Puzzle

"Really, Rudolpho, I'm getting suspicious! Every time we go out I end up paying. Just how many castles do you have, anyway?"

"Don't be a silly little goose, ma chère! A third of my castles are in France. A fifth are in Spain and three times the difference of these two totals are the number I have in Austria. Also, my mother lives in one in Italy. The total number of my castles is less than twenty. Now, could I have an extra 200 francs for carfare?"

Just how many castles in the air does Rudolpho "own" anyway? And should Millicent give him the 200 francs?

World's Most Perplexing "Radio" Puzzle

"Radio Dog! Fetch the Royal Executioner!"

"Ali Babel here with another round of your favorite riddle show, 'What's the Difference?' To start off:
'What's the difference between our king and a rejected lover?'
'What's the difference between our king and a flea?'
'What's the difference between a hungry man and our king?' "

When early radio came to the Middle East a lot of people lost their heads over it. The above short-lived program is a perfect example. Do you know the answers to Ali's kingly riddles?

World's Most Perplexing "Law Court" Puzzle

"And furthermore, my lord, the defense will show that when the decedent, Bottles Bremmerton, challenged the defendant to identify the notable person in the following poetic puzzle:

'Five hundred begins it, five hundred ends it,
    Five in the middle is seen;
The first of all figures, the first of all letters,
    Take up their stations between.
Join all together, and then you will bring
    Before you the name of an eminent king,'

he did so with the intent to ridicule and humiliate my client. We will show that after badgering my client every day in front of his friends at the Yard-of-Ale public house, my client suffered a brainstorm that resulted in the subsequent stein-throwing incident, which led to the accidental bashing in of Bottles Bremmerton's brains with a Winston Churchill toby mug."

Barrister Hugh Standforth has an uphill fight on his hands. While he finishes his opening statement can you solve the problem that led to the demise of Bottles Bremmerton?

World's Most Perplexing "Detective" Puzzle

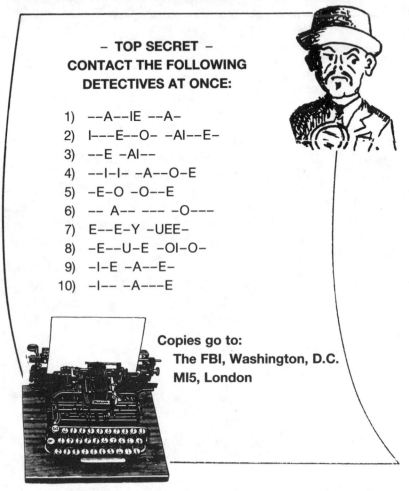

- TOP SECRET -
CONTACT THE FOLLOWING
DETECTIVES AT ONCE:

1) --A--IE --A-
2) I---E--O- -AI--E-
3) --E -AI--
4) --I-I- -A--O-E
5) -E-O -O--E
6) -- A-- --- -O---
7) E--E-Y -UEE-
8) -E--U-E -OI-O-
9) -I-E -A--E-
10) -I-- -A---E

Copies go to:
The FBI, Washington, D.C.
MI5, London

When the new hundred-dollar bill printing plates disappeared from the U.S. mint, word went out to the world's ten top detectives. Their names above are encoded using the secret vowel code. Only the vowels in their names are printed. The first is Charlie Chan. Can you decipher the remaining nine?

World's Most Perplexing "Automaton" Puzzle

$$AB + CD + (EF/GH) + (I/J) = 100$$

Pictured above is the famous Victorian automaton "Psycho." The mechanical wonder is trying to solve the number-substitution problem in the frame. The puzzler is required to substitute the ten digits 0 to 9 for the letters so a true equation is formed. Each digit can only be used once. See if you can crank out the answer before "Psycho."

World's Most Perplexing "Anagrams" Puzzles

"Look, dear, this painting is by your favorite artist, 'I Paint Modern.'"

The above charming drawing illustrates a flying trip through an extensive art museum. The gentleman at the top, pointing out a particular painting to his companion, has playfully transformed the artist's name into an anagram. In an anagram, you take the letters in a word or name, and rearrange them to form other names or words that, ideally, have something in common with the original word. The answer to the one here is "Piet Mondrian." Try your skills at unscrambling the examples below:

1) To love ruin = ?
2) Great help = ?
3) Govern, clever lad! = ?
4) Hated for ill = ?
5) Flit on, cheering angel! = ?
6) Old West action = ?
7) Name for ship = ?

World's Most Perplexing "Hopping" Puzzle

"All right, gents, belly up to the starting line. The race course runs straight ahead to the old oak tree. When you reach it you are to turn around and head back to the starting line. The first one to cross it wins the race. On your mark, get set, start hopping!"

The course measured twelve feet from the starting line to the old oak tree, so the total length of the race was twenty-four feet. According to the morning line, the grasshopper could cover ten inches during a single hop while the little frog could only cover six inches per hop. However, since the frog could hop five times for every three hops of the grasshopper, he stayed neck in neck with him down the course. Despite being so evenly matched, when they reached the finish line one of them crossed it ahead of the other. Who took home the trophy?

World's Most Perplexing "Puzzle Platters" Puzzle

"What fun being able to play word games at the beach! Try this one, Wharton:
    'My first I hope you are,
    My second I see you are,
    Put them together for something I know you are.'"

"This new record must contain over a hundred word charades. See if you can fathom this one while I take a dip!
    'My first is a way to travel.
    My second is something people often lie about.
    Combined, it's something tasty but aromatic.'"

"My first is a sailor,
My second's to gain,
My whole, though oft shot at,
Has never been slain."

A sunny day at the beach with your best girl, a portable gramophone, and a stack of puzzle platters. What bliss! Back in the 1920's, puzzles even came on records. See if you can solve the above three puzzles.

World's Most Perplexing "Christmas Stocking" Puzzle

Let's see, now, this year we have two sizes of stocking for the children. We have the "I've been good" size and the "I've been very good" size! Why, bless me, I see a puzzle here. The number of toys in the large stocking is equal to the number in the small stocking reversed. And the difference between the amounts in each is one-eleventh the sum of the two amounts. My, my!

How many toys are in each stocking?

World's Most Perplexing "Bottle" Puzzle

"I so hate being sick in bed. There's so little to do. Now, Doctor Stall bet me I couldn't make up a puzzle that dealt with medicine. Those two bottles give me an idea. Suppose a man is alone on an island and is bitten by a poisonous snake and only has ten minutes before it takes effect. He has with him a bottle three-quarters full of an antidote. He also has an identical empty bottle. However, he must only take half a bottle of antidote. Less or more would be fatal. How can he measure out exactly the right amount using only the two bottles for pouring? That problem should stump the old sawbones!"

You can't keep a good puzzler down, as exemplified here by Aunt Hattie. Just how did the young man in her story manage to measure out exactly half a bottle of medicine to save his life?

World's Most Perplexing "Riddles" Puzzles

"Which letter is like a Roman emperor?"

"Which candles burn longer—wax or tallow?"

"Who was the most successful physician in the Bible?"

"What is eaten at breakfast or lunch, but usually drunk only at dinner?"

"What kind of grain is usually sown at night?"

The above streetcar is heading out of town to the "1927 International Puzzle Fair" being held at Olympic Park, New Jersey. The riders are all entered in the riddle contest. Hop on board and try your luck!

World's Most Perplexing "Nails" Puzzle

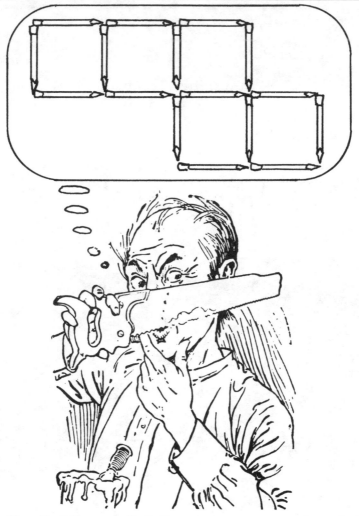

Old Charlie "Crosscut" Callaway, proprietor of our local lumberyard, is having a hard time concentrating on his morning shave. The boys in the warehouse bet him he couldn't move four nails in the above setup to new positions to make six squares instead of five. See if you can hammer out the answer before starting time.

World's Most Perplexing "Soap Opera" Puzzle

What's going on here? Is this a new Reformation sitcom, "The Not So Young and Restless"? Can you explain the significance of the above tableau?

World's Most Perplexing "Echophone" Puzzle

The one toy the Cathcart kids loved above all else was their Echophone. Each of the 19 children owned one record cylinder that contained a short bedtime story. They kept the recordings in a special record case. One day Uncle Mohr noted that the record slots were connected by 12 bars, six around the outside and six spokes around the center. Each bar connected three slots. "Here's a puzzle," he said. "See if you can place the 19 numbered records in the slots in such a manner that the sum of any three record values along a bar will add up to 23."

The reader is invited to make a copy of the record case and play along with Uncle Mohr.

World's Most Perplexing "Picture" Puzzle

Back on page 70 we introduced you to word square puzzles. Here's a second one for you to work on. Lay out a grid with four letters across and four letters down. Hints concerning the four words needed to solve the puzzle are in the above picture of a circuit rider minister in the Old West preaching to his flock.

World's Most Perplexing "Tattoo" Puzzle

"Puzzle Tattoos" were Mr. Quinlan's specialty. Make an enlarged drawing of the "13" puzzle pictured above and place 12 coins on the circles, leaving the center one empty. Now, remove 11 of them by jumping one over another, as in checkers. The last coin must end up on the center circle.

World's Most Perplexing "Addition" Puzzle

> *"Don't turn around! You numbskulls have had five minutes to write down the correct solution on the blackboard to that simple problem! I give you five more seconds!"*

Professor Nebelwerfer is about to live up to his name (it means rocket launcher). In five seconds the Inkerman twins will lift off the floor. The Herr Professor has rather a unique way of showing his displeasure with dunderheads. The problem that has caused consternation for Hans and Fedor is as follows: Arrange five odd digits in such a way that they add up to 20. The same odd digit can be used more than once. You also have five minutes to solve this one.

World's Most Perplexing "Clown" Puzzles

"Beware! I, Baffles, am about to bombastically bother both bright and befuddled bystanders!"

"Can anyone tell me what two whole numbers when multiplied together equal 31?"

"How many esses appear in the name of the longest river in the world?"

"If I were to give 15 cents to this young man and 10 cents to this young lady, what time of the day would it be?"

World's Most Perplexing "Collar" Puzzle

This puzzle is similar to the "Santa" problem on page 60. The above board is laid out using 13 celluloid collars and 12 miscellaneous items from a Victorian kitchen. In the pattern every other square contains a collar. The problem is to cut the board into four pieces that can then be put together to form two smaller boards, one with four squares to a side and the other with three squares to a side. You must cut along the lines of the grid that divides the board. The two new boards must maintain the same pattern as the original board with every other square, horizontally and vertically, containing a collar.

World's Most Perplexing "Diner" Puzzle

Come and join us at our favorite diner in Bloomfield, New Jersey. Hash House Harriet is calling out an order using the colorful mode of speech employed in this type of eatery. We've arranged the sentence to form an interesting puzzle for you to solve. If you replace each letter with a number, using the same number for the same letter wherever it appears, you can make a correct mathematical expression out of her order. Also, can you figure out what the order is for?

World's Most Perplexing "Puzzle Poker" Puzzle

"Sabilla, I'll bet you $100 you can't solve this triangle card puzzle in less than five minutes!"

"Really, Zoë, when will you ever learn! I'll see that $100 and raise you $200 more!"

In "Puzzle Poker" the players wager on each other's ability to solve pasteboard problems. Using the cards ace through nine of diamonds, Zoë has dealt out a card triangle on the table. The problem for Sabilla is to rearrange the cards so that the total number of pips of any four cards that make up the three sides of the triangle will add up to 23. The value of each corner card will appear in two sides.

To take the pot from these ladies the reader will have to solve the puzzle in less than four minutes!

World's Most Perplexing "Automobile" Puzzle

> "Well, Highpockets, you certainly look pleased with yourself. You must have unloaded one of those tin lizzies on some unsuspecting boob!"

> "They're called antique classics, my dear, and I unloaded, er, sold two of them. I got $21,000 for the pair from that ne'er-do-well Malcolm Dolittle. I made a ten percent profit on the 1931 Duesenberg. However, I had to take a ten percent loss on the 1929 Packard Speedster. Still, I was glad to get rid of it. All told, I made a profit of five percent on the sale of the two cars. How about helping me celebrate with dinner at El Morocco?"

"Highpockets" Anderson catered to the automotive needs of New York society, whether they were on the way up or on the way down. Can you figure out how much he originally paid for each of the vintage cars?

World's Most Perplexing "Maze" Puzzle

The above maze is probably the most famous one con-
structed in the 19th century. Created by Lewis Carroll to
amuse his brothers and sisters, it is extremely devious.
The paths go in and out, over and under, and contain
many dead-ends. Can you get to the center of the maze
in time to save Mr. Dumpty from falling?

World's Most Perplexing "Dancing" Puzzle

"Elsie, you're so light on your feet tonight. Do you know that we've covered one-fifth of the Marathon's distance already?"

"Oh, Ambrose, I could go on like this all night. Why don't we dance one mile an hour faster! If we did that, we would cut a full hour off the time it took us to dance this contest last week!"

Back in the Roaring Twenties marathon dancing was a craze that knew no bounds. The particular contest that our ardent dancers are participating in was a "Distance Dance." Each couple was fitted with an pedometer to measure the distance they had danced. From the facts given above can you determine the length of the marathon to be danced?

World's Most Perplexing "Sock Sale" Puzzle

The time is 1902 and Davenport Department Store is having its great Holiday Sock Sale! The one collaring the hapless sales clerk with her umbrella is Aunt Hattie. For only $8.00 Hattie was able to purchase the last 20 pairs of socks in the store. She paid $1.60 a pair for some very nice long winter socks, 20¢ a pair for calf-high socks, and 10¢ a pair for children's short socks. How many pairs of each type of socks did Aunt Hattie buy?

Judging by the above picture, little has changed over the years when it comes to shopping at Christmastime.

World's Most Perplexing "Telegraphers" Puzzle

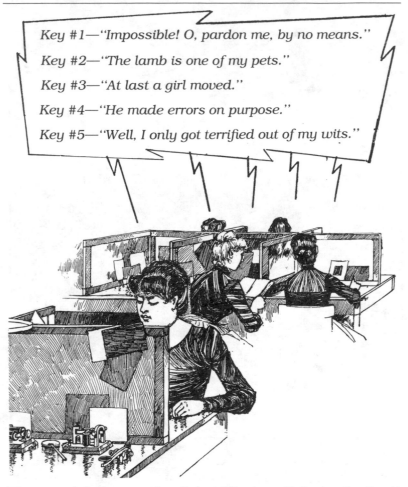

Key #1—"Impossible! O, pardon me, by no means."

Key #2—"The lamb is one of my pets."

Key #3—"At last a girl moved."

Key #4—"He made errors on purpose."

Key #5—"Well, I only got terrified out of my wits."

The young ladies at the Great Western Telegraphy Institute are practicing for their final exams. When they can send three "hidden word" sentences in one minute, their futures in communications will be assured. Hidden in each of the above sentences are the names of one or more animals. As an example, here's how you might hide the word "pig" in a sentence: "I must give it up, I grieve to say."

World's Most Perplexing "Enigma" Puzzle

"My first you will be,
   If you're good and upright.
My second you'll see
   In a sharp, frosty night.
Together combined,
   I'm a virtue that's great,
That should govern each mind,
   And preside in each state
'Now, mosey on up to the bar and name your poison. If the defendant can solve the riddle I just propounded I'll let him off with time served and a round of drinks for the court! Miss it, and spend 30 days in the lockup!' "

Here we see Judge Roy Bean, the "only law west of the Pecos," about to try Pegleg Patterson for a breach of the law. The answer to this riddle has something to do with Roy's profession.

World's Most Perplexing "Dictionary" Puzzle

For those of you who enjoy word puzzles we present the old dictionary quiz. Above are illustrations taken from a very old dictionary. Below are listed seventeen words, twelve of which describe the illustrated items. Can you match them up?

A) Generatrix   F) Obelisk   J) Colophon   N) Moulage

B) Dirk   G) Coupe   K) Shako   O) Deadeyes

C) Shroud   H) Arbalest   L) Tetrapylon   P) Hippogriff

D) Ballista   I) Oubliette   M) Scarab   Q) Pediment

E) Aboma

World's Most Perplexing "Key Holder" Puzzle

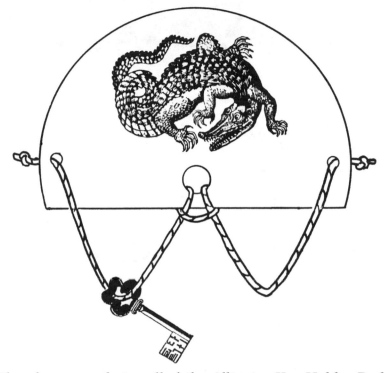

The above puzzle is called the Alligator Key Holder Problem. The materials needed to make it are a piece of cardboard, some string, and an old key. Cut the cardboard to roughly the shape and size of the one in our diagram. Make two small holes on either side of it just large enough to poke the ends of the string through. Make a larger hole in the middle of the cardboard. The hole must be too small for the key to pass through. Cut off a piece of string about twelve inches long, thread it through the key and the holes in the cardboard, and knot the two ends. You should have no difficulty duplicating the setup in our picture. The puzzle is to transfer the key from the left-hand loop to the right-hand loop. This puzzle is very old, but still very good.

World's Most Perplexing "Lunch Tray" Puzzle

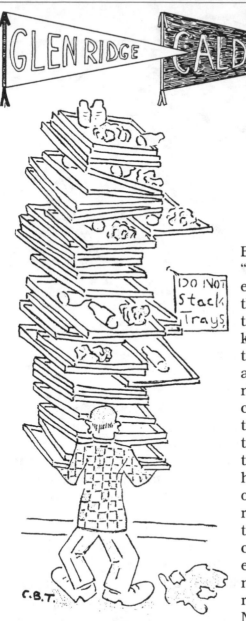

Back in high school "Muscles" Moran made extra money by taking the other kids' empty trays back to the kitchen. He charged them a nickel a tray and was famed for the number of trays he could carry at one time. One day he returned 99 trays in only two trips. When asked how many he carried on each of the trips, he replied, "Two-thirds the number of trays I carried on my first trip equals four-fifths the number of trays I carried on my second trip. Now, you figure it out!"

ANSWERS

"Curtailing" Puzzles (page 6). The answers are: 1) GRAVEL-GRAVE; 2) COVERT-COVER; 3) HAIRY-HAIR; 4) MARK-MAR; 5) INCOMER-INCOME; 6) HIDE-HID; 7) PINK-PIN. For those of you who took the bait and lost, your next word is "hello."

"Math Signs" Puzzle (page 7). There is more than one answer to this problem. Here's one of them:

$$123 - 45 - 67 + 89 = 100$$

"Bolt" Puzzle (page 8). The heads of the bolts remain the same distance apart regardless of the direction you rotate them in.

"Cleaning" Puzzle (page 9). One man can do the job in 3 hours and 40 minutes. Although it takes one man 7 hours and 20 minutes to do 30 windows, he has to clean *both* sides of each window. When cleaning a mirror, however, he only has to clean one side of the glass. Therefore, the time it takes to do a mirror is half that of a window.

"Tin Man" Puzzle (page 10). Starting with the "I" at the top right of the frame, read around the frame counterclockwise. The famous quote is, "It's better to wear out than to rust out!" The quote is by Richard Cumberland (from Boswell's *Tour of the Hebrides*).

"Hidden Towns" Puzzle (page 11). The first location is Annapolis: "How *Anna polis*hes the silver when Jack is expected."

The second is Fairhaven: "Such little puffs o*f air have n*o effect on the yachts."

"Treasure" Puzzle (page 12). What clues can we find in order to work this problem? First, there are no three-letter English words that do not contain at least one vowel. On examining the dials we find that "*Y*," on the middle dial, is the only vowel to be found. Next, the secret combination word has something to do with the owner of the chest, the bishop of Bristol. There is just such a three-letter word, "*PYX*." The dictionary defines pyx as "a box or vessel in which the reserved Eucharist or Host is kept."

"Chocolate" Puzzle (page 13). Piece *A* alone forms the first square. Then the two pieces marked *B* fit together to form the second. Next, the two pieces marked *C* make up the third square; and, finally, the four pieces marked *D* can be used to form the fourth square.

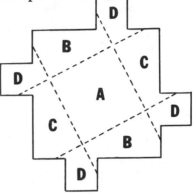

"Spaceship" Puzzle (page 14). (See drawing.)

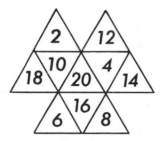

"Lightning Calculator" Puzzle (page 15). The answer is simplicity itself. The two-inch piece of plastic (or a wooden match) when placed on the grid horizontally or vertically will cover six numbers. Upon trying this out you will note that the first and last number of any line or column so covered will be the same. You have only to add this number to 65 and you will have the sum of the six numbers in question. As an example, place the stick on line two, starting with the second number from the left. The stick will cover numbers 17, 9, 21, 13, 5, and 17. The sum of these six numbers is 82. Note that both the first and last number in this line of six numbers is 17. If you add 17 to 65 you get 82, the sum in question.

As for placing the stick diagonally on the grid, it will always cover only five numbers, and the sum of these numbers will *always* be 65. So save the diagonal part of the puzzle for last since obviously it can not be repeated. For a dramatic finish, turn your back to the table, write your "prediction" on a piece of paper, fold it up, and hand it to someone in your audience before the match is placed diagonally on the grid. When your prediction has been proven correct, pocket the numbered card and go on to your next puzzle so no one is given the opportunity to examine the grid and perhaps learn the secret of your powers.

"Animal" Puzzle (page 16). The eight animal collective nouns are:

    1) A doylt of swine.
    2) A gaggle of geese.
    3) A rout of wolves.
    4) A troop of monkeys.
    5) A leap of leopards.
    6) A skulk of foxes.
    7) A sloth of bears.
    8) A muster of peacocks.

"Match" Puzzle (page 17). Remove two corner matches from the upper-right and bottom-left corners and the four matches from the inside of the figure. You now have one small square and two large squares, for a total of three squares.

"Domino" Puzzle (page 18). Here are the six other squares that we know about.

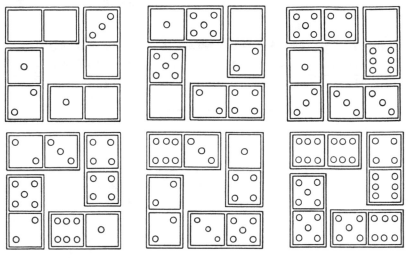

"Line" Puzzle (page 19). To solve this problem you must start and stop the line at a junction where three parts of the line come together. In the drawing below, these parts are above the Bard's right eye and on his left shoulder next to his collar and hair.

"Card" Puzzle (page 20). This is really a fine wager and one that you can do over and over gain. The secret to always winning is to make sure that the bottom cards of the two halves of the deck are *red and black* before you shuffle the cards together. Also, a stipulation for the wager is that you can only shuffle the deck *once!* If you adhere to these two rules, all the pairs you turn over will have one red card and one black card and you will win $26.00. You can't ask for a better bet!

"Hidden Face" Puzzle (page 21). Rotate the picture of the fairgoers a quarter turn counterclockwise. Look to the right of the brim on Hiram's hat to see the face of the boarder looking to the left.

"Magic Square" Puzzle (page 22). The following answer shows one way of distributing the numbers around the sides of the square.

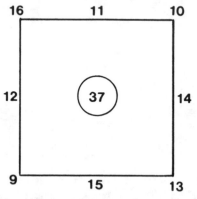

"Cross" Puzzle (page 23). Make two cuts across the cross as indicated below. Next, reassemble them as shown in the second drawing.

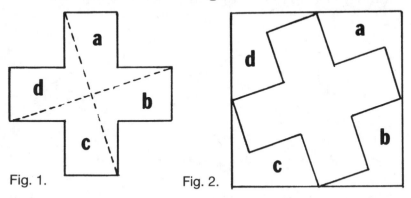

Fig. 1.   Fig. 2.

"What, When, and Why" Puzzles (page 24). 1) It is matchless. 2) When it is scaled. 3) Because a good batter makes good dough. 4) One is hard to get up and the other is hard to get down. 5) When it is a skylight. 6) Because she has a head on one side and a tail on the other. 7) Ohio.

"Betting" Puzzle (page 25). The amazing thing about this betting proposition is that it works itself. Let's review the action. You take 20 cards from the top of the deck and turn them face-up. You then shuffle these cards back into the deck and hand it to your victim, who can riffle-shuffle it or overhand shuffle it as many times as he chooses. When he's done he counts off the top 20 cards, squares them into a deck, and hands them to you under the table. He then places the remainder of the deck on top of the table. You have no way of knowing how many of the cards in the remaining deck of 32 are face-up. Also, there is no way for you to distinguish which cards in your hand are face-up and face-down. How are you going to win the bet? Easily! Just turn the deck over in your hands. Then, for effect, pretend to be turning cards over and moving them around under the table. Tell your audience that your fingers are so sensitive that you can feel if a card is face-up or face-down. As for knowing how many cards are face-up in the deck on the table, tell them that it's a mental gift you were born with.

Now, bring the deck out from under the table and place it next to the remaining deck of 32 cards and invite the person you made the wager with to count the number of face-up cards in each deck. They will be the same. The number of face-up cards should vary each time you perform this feat.

A word of caution: When your opponent divides the deck before shuffling, make sure he doesn't turn one of the halves over. This is the only move that could cause the trick to fail.

"Fireworks" Puzzle (page 26). There were

Seven joke bottle corks	@ $0.01 =	$0.07
Seven Towers of Gold	@ $0.05 =	$0.35
Ten Laughing Uncles	@ $0.10 =	$1.00
Four Comical Nut Crackers	@ $0.25 =	$1.00
	Total . . .	$2.42

"Archaeology" Puzzle (page 27). If you look closely at Hawking's picture of Bacchus, god of wine, you will find that the portrait's features and flowing beard are really made up of two people, a handsome youth and a pretty, young lady, caught in the act of kissing and embracing. The intoxicating nectar of young love used to portray the slightly inebriated visage of ancient revelry.

"Aces and Kings" Puzzle (page 28). The setup of the eight cards, from the top down, in the deck is ace, king, king, ace, king, king, ace, ace. This is with the deck turned face-down.

"Book" Puzzle (page 30). The mystery was finally solved with the arrival of Algernon, the library's clerk. His explanation went something like this:

"Gee, what an easy puzzle that is, Pops. I learned it in sixth grade. Take a strong paper bag and lay it on the table with the open end hanging over the edge. Next, place the books on top of the other end of the bag. Now all you have to do is to blow into the open end of the bag while making sure that you keep the bag tight against your mouth so that none of the air escapes. A couple of good puffs and the books will tilt up and fall over. Didn't you guys learn anything in school?"

"Checker" Puzzle (page 31). Black to move and win: 11–16, 19–15, 22–18, 14–23, 16–19, 23–16, 12–10, 3–8, 10–7. White is now trapped, making black the winner.

"Toothpick" Puzzle (page 32). Move the three toothpicks on the extreme right of the original setup to the new positions indicated below. You now have 9 small squares, 4 medium-sized squares made up of 4 squares each, and 1 large square made up of the 9 small squares. It's reported that Roderick Sneakwell failed this test. Would you have won a Dusty Road cone?

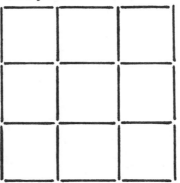

"Cardboard" Puzzle (page 33). Cut along the lines indicated in the first drawing and remove the small center piece. Next, revolve the small piece 180 degrees and place it back against the larger piece as indicated in the second drawing. You now have a two-foot square of cardboard with a one-foot-square hole in the center.

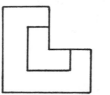

"Sandwich" Puzzle (page 34). The total number of watercress, asparagus, and cucumber sandwiches needed to satisfy the problem is 121.

"Rebus" Puzzle (page 35). Rebus #1—"You can come out later, Mr. *Jack-in-the-box!*" (knave inside a carton)

Rebus #2—"My next selection will be *Schubert's Unfinished Symphony!*"

Rebus #3—"Not on your *tintype,* Mr. Belows!" ("T" in the word "type" becomes tintype.)

"Racing" Puzzle (page 36). The following is only one of many solutions to this problem.

6	5	4	3	2	1
5	3	1	6	4	2
4	1	2	5	6	3
3	6	5	2	1	4
2	4	6	1	3	5
1	2	3	4	5	6

"Synonym" Puzzle (page 37). The winning synonyms were 1) quilt; 2) query; 3) quite; 4) quack; 5) quail; 6) queue; 7) quart; 8) queen; 9) quick; 10) quark; 11) quill; 12) qualm; 13) quest; 14) quiet; 15) quota; 16) quell; 17) quash; 18) quaff; 19) quake; 20) quirt.

"Age" Puzzle (page 38). Well, it looks as though old Bartlett really does have an eye for the younger ladies. Using Heloise's formula, she has to be 18 years old. If she's 18 today, then three times her age three years from now would be 63, and three times her age three years ago would be 45. Now, 63 − 45 = 18.

"Grand Prize" Puzzle (page 39). Winthrop won the day by observing that each of the numbers above the line is spelled with three letters. Since the next number in the sequence, 10, is also spelled with three letters, Winthrop correctly ascertained that the number should go above the line. Another trophy for his collection.

"Watch" Puzzle (page 40). For all three watches again to register the correct time at noon it will be necessary for the watch that is losing one minute every 24 hours to lose 12 hours and for the other watch to gain 12 hours. At the rate of one minute a day this will occur in exactly 720 days.

"Checking" Puzzle (page 41). Mr. Bender's original check was for $15.35. The bartender gave him $35.15 in cash. After paying his bar tab, $4.45, he had $30.70 left, which is just twice the amount of the check.

"Rearranging" Puzzle (page 42). The cities visited are:

TCLTUACA = CALCUTTA
RZIBRTIA = BIARRITZ
OULHNULO = HONOLULU
TENAWCOP = CAPE TOWN
YVRIKEKAJ = REYKJAVIK
GESPRIANO = SINGAPORE
TRHMUPTOOS = PORTSMOUTH
LENUMEOBR = MELBOURNE
BNACSAALAC = CASABLANCA
ORNONAG = RANGOON
SSRFACONCAIN = SAN FRANCISCO
NKGNGHOO = HONG KONG

"Millennium" Puzzle (page 43). For those of you who couldn't solve it and who can't wait until the year 2000 we give the following solution. By the way, this square isn't limited to the ways of totaling 2000 that we mentioned earlier. The four center squares and the four corner squares also add up to 2000. Also, the four squares that make up the four quadrants of the square. There are also a couple of other ways for making 2000. See if you can find them.

499	502	507	492
506	493	498	503
494	509	500	497
501	496	495	508

"Ancient" Puzzle (page 44). When in Rome, do as the Romans do . . . and use the Roman numbering system. One-third of TWELVE (the word) would be the two letters LV, which equals 55. Also, one-fifth of SEVEN (the word) is the single letter V, which equals 5. So, LV $\div$ V = 55 $\div$ 5 = 11.

"Insect" Puzzle (page 45). The eight insects we came up with are ANT, FLEA, FLY, GNAT, LICE, MITE, MOTH, WASP.

"Electricity" Puzzle (page 46). While the secret is very simple it's the presentation that will make or break this mystery. First, find the center of the card by drawing two diagonal lines from corner to corner. Next, bend the two corners as shown, one corner up and the other corner down. Now, balance the card on the point of the pin. Give the card a spin with one finger. Do not set it spinning by blowing on it. This would give the secret away.

When the card has stopped spinning, pretend to build up a charge of static electricity in your body by scuffing your shoes on the rug and rubbing the tops of your fingers with a silk scarf or some other type of cloth. Now, cup your hands and bring them up close to the card. As you do this, caution everyone not to move lest they stir up the air. Move your hands about slowly and lean over the card. Open your lips slightly and gently breathe down towards the card. Your breath will either hit the card directly or bounce off your cupped hands, setting the card spinning on the needle. With practice you will be able to start and stop the spinning and even be able to cause it to revolve in opposite directions.

After you've successfully demonstrated your "Paper Motor," step and back watch the fun as your audience tries to make the card spin as you did.

"Triangle" Puzzle (page 47). The dashes denote the three rods that must be removed from the figure. You are then left with three small triangles, three medium-sized triangles, and the seventh large triangle that contains the rest. After all, the young lady *didn't* specify that the seven remaining triangles would all be the same size.

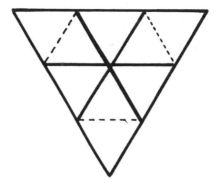

"Change-the-Word" Puzzle (page 48). With this type of puzzle you're more than likely to come up with one or more different answers. We give you the ones that we are familiar with.

1) BOAT, COAT, COST, CAST, CASH
2) STAR, SEAR, FEAR, FEAT, FEET
3) ROAD, GOAD, GOAL, COAL, COIL
4) BELL, SELL, SILL, SILT, SIFT
5) CALL, MALL, MALE, MATE, MUTE
6) RAFT, RANT, RANG, RING, WING

"Dog House" Puzzle (page 49). The dotted lines indicate the matches moved.

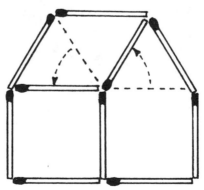

"Chickenman" Puzzle (page 54). The answer to the Chickenman's puzzle is the number 8.

"Barber" Puzzle (page 55). Each pair of scissors cost the salesman $6.00. If he sold one pair for $9.00, then his profit was $3.00. If he sold two pair for $15.00 and they cost him $12.00 to buy, then his profit would still be $3.00. So, either way, the salesman stood to make $3.00 on the sale.

"Christmas" Puzzle (page 56). Let's hope Santa was extra generous with these birthday kids. On Christmas morn Barton was 8, Wendel was 5, and Susan was 3.

"Number" Puzzle (page 57). Send Professor Flunkum back to class with the following solution:

$$
\begin{array}{r}
2\ 1\ 9\ 7\ 8 \\
\times\ 4 \\
\hline
8\ 7\ 9\ 1\ 2
\end{array}
$$

"Archery" Puzzle (page 58). The villainous sore loser Hayward Nottingham was right about the puzzle. With the target they were using it was impossible to score 21 with six arrows. However, the Hood sisters were well aware of that old trick and knew how to solve it. Roberta put three arrows in the "1" circle and Carmella put three arrows in the "9" circle. Roberta then turned the target upside down, which left the value of the "1" circle still 1, but changed the value of the "9" circle to 6. The total of the six hits then came to 21. After that, Nottingham quit the club and took up skeet shooting.

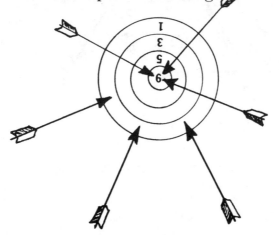

"Magic Kettle" Puzzle (page 59). Since there are 35 heads, the minimum number of legs would be 70 (two for each bird). The farmer said the total number of legs was 94, which means that we have an extra 24 legs. Dividing the extra legs by 2 we get 12, the number of four-legged animals in the rabbit cage. Since we now know that 12 of the animals were rabbits, it follows that there were 23 pheasants in the other cage.

"Santa" Puzzle (page 60). Take a pencil and ruler and divide the square into 25 smaller squares, as shown in figure 1. Now, cut the square into four smaller pieces (cut along the heavy lines). We've numbered these four segments 1 through 4. If you now reassemble these four segments as indicated in figures 2 and 3, you will have two squares, each with a complete Santa.

Fig. 1

Fig. 2

"Pentagram" Puzzle (page 61). This is the one solution to this puzzle that we are aware of.

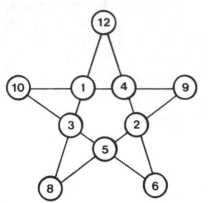

"Blacksmith" Puzzle (page 62).

"Solid Shape" Puzzle (page 63). The six shapes called for by Merlin are 1) a ball; 2) a cone; 3) a cylinder; 4) a three-sided pyramid; 5) a four-sided pyramid; 6) a cube. Now let's get back and find out what in the world an infinite-sided solid is.

"Tailors" Puzzle (page 64). We know that Nathan and Saul sat on the same kind of seat. We also know that Saul and David sat on different types of seats. Finally, we know that Ira sat on a different type of seat from David, so Ira's must have been of the same type as Nathan and Saul's. Therefore, Nathan, Saul, and Ira all sat on the same type of seat, the stools. David and Abe sat on the two chairs. I hope that you didn't get cuffed around by that puzzle.

"Musical" Puzzle (page 65). Number the seven notes 1 through 7 as indicated in the drawing below. If you invert the following notes, in three moves, you will end up with all seven notes right side up. Turn notes 1, 2, and 3; then turn 3, 4, and 5; then turn 3, 6, and 7.

"Doctor" Puzzle (page 66). The solution to this one rests in telling time. Eleven plus two equals one if the time is eleven o'clock and you add two hours to it, thus changing the time to one o'clock. Doctor Stall gave you a hint how to solve it when he stated that no army man could solve it. In the military if you added two hours to eleven o'clock, the new time would be thirteen hundred hours.

"Color" Puzzle (page 67).
    1) On the ocean—*White*cap
    2) A first starter—*Green*horn
    3) Found in pies—*Black*bird
    4) Some find it tasty—*Blue*grass
    5) A type of building—*Brown*stone
    6) Lacking in sense—*Dun*ce
    7) The ape man—*Grey*stoke
    8) Best in the shade—*Lemon*ade
    9) An unpleasant sight—*Pink*eye
    10) A strong liquid—*Red*eye

"Reverse Word" Puzzle (page 68). 1) The form of exercise is *STEP* exercise. Reverse the spelling of it and you get your best friends, your *PETS*.

2) If you get out of the frying *PAN* you'll be in the fire. Reverse this and you'll take a *NAP* on the cot.

3) In *MAY* we dance until we're beat. Reverse this and the treat you'll dig up will be a *YAM*, or sweet potato.

"Apple" Puzzle (page 69). Sy gave each of his first five sons an apple from the basket. There was then one apple left in the basket. Sy then gave the basket with the apple in it to his sixth son. As the puzzle stated, Sy divided the six apples equally among his sons, and one apple was left in the basket.

"Word Square" Puzzle (page 70). The five words are: 1) *SATED;* 2) *ATONE;* 3) *TOAST;* 4) *ENSUE;* 5) *DETER.*

```
S A T E D
A T O N E
T O A S T
E N S U E
D E T E R
```

"Poetry" Puzzle (page 71). This is one of those puzzles you have to work backwards to solve. First off, six score plus ten equals 120 + 10, or 130. Now, 3 times 3 equals 9, so let's subtract 9 from 130, giving us 121. The last two figures we have to subtract from this amount are one half and one third of his original age. Looking for a common denominator we come up with 6/6 for his original age. Half of that is 3/6, and a third of that is 2/6. So, the 121 equals 6/6 plus 3/6 plus 2/6, or, 11/6. If we divide 121 by 11 we get the 1/6, which equals 11. So Oswald's current age, 6/6, would come to 66, an amount that would clearly make him a spent buck in Philomena's eyes.

"Sphinx" Puzzle (page 72). The drawing below shows the arrangement of the four little "Sphinxlets" within the original Sphinx.

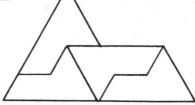

"Castle" Puzzle (page 73). Rudolpho claims he has 15 castles. Millicent should keep the money and let Rudolpho hoof it back to town.

"Radio" Puzzle (page 74). 1) What's the difference between our king and a rejected lover? Our king kisses his missus, and the other misses his kisses.

2) What's the difference between our king and a flea? Our king can have fleas, but a flea can't have our king.

3) What's the difference between a hungry man and our king? A hungry man longs to eat while our king eats too long.

"Law Court" Puzzle (page 75). The person of royalty described in the puzzle is King David. The five hundred that begins and ends it is the Roman numeral *D*. Also, the five in the middle is the Roman numeral *V*. The first of all letters in the alphabet is *A*, and the first figure is one, or *I* in Roman numerals.

"Detective" Puzzle (page 76). The detectives are: 1) Charlie Chan; 2) Inspector Maigret; 3) The Saint; 4) Philip Marlowe; 5) Nero Wolfe; 6) Mr. and Mrs. North; 7) Ellery Queen; 8) Hercule Poirot; 9) Mike Hammer; 10) Miss Marple.

"Automaton" Puzzle (page 77). There are several answers to this excellent puzzle. Here are the two that "Psycho" came up with:
$$17 + 82 + (45/90) + (3/6) = 100$$
$$49 + 50 + (38/76) + (1/2) = 100$$

"Anagrams" Puzzles (page 78). 1) Revolution; 2) Telegraph; 3) Grover Cleveland; 4) Adolf Hitler; 5) Florence Nightingale; 6) Clint Eastwood; 7) HMS Pinafore

"Hopping" Puzzle (page 79). The first to cross the finish line was . . . the little frog. Here's how he did it: Although they stayed neck in neck down the course, when they reached the oak tree the frog's twenty-fourth hop landed him exactly on the twelve-foot line while the grasshopper's fifteenth hop sent him six inches beyond the line. At this point they both turned around and started hopping back to the starting line. However, since the fog now had a six-inch lead over the grasshopper he easily beat him when they came down to the finish line.

"Puzzle Platters" Puzzle (page 80).
1) Welcome (well-come)
2) Cabbage (cab-age)
3) Target (tar-get)

"Christmas Stocking" Puzzle (page 81). There were 54 toys in the larger stocking and 45 toys in the smaller. The 54 is the reverse of 45. The sum of the toys in the two stockings is 99, and one-eleventh of that number is 9, the difference between the number of toys in the two stockings.

"Bottle" Puzzle (page 82). Hattie's poisoned puzzler quickly picked up a handful of pebbles, of varying sizes, and started dropping them into the bottle that contained the antidote. When the liquid reached the neck of the bottle the volume of liquid displaced by the pebbles equalled one-fourth the volume of the bottle. He then poured the antidote into the empty bottle until the level of liquid was the same in both bottles. The second bottle now contained exactly half a bottle of antidote, which saved his life and enabled Aunt Hattie to be one up on old Doc Stall.

"Riddles" Puzzles (page 83).
1) P—because it is near 0 (Nero).
2) Neither; both burn shorter.
3) Job; he had the most patience.
4) Toast.
5) Wild oats.

"Nails" Puzzle (page 84). If you move the nails indicated by the dash lines to the positions shown below, you will end up with five small squares and one large square, for a total of six.

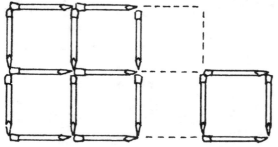

"Soap Opera" Puzzle (page 85). Reformation, yes; soap opera, no. The three characters in our picture are merely practicing for an evening's entertainment down at the Bottle and Blades Tavern. Every Wednesday night is puzzle night and they're entered in the "Palindromes Contest." A palindrome is a word or line that reads the same backwards and forward. If you check the three sentences in our picture you will see that they are all palindromes.

"Echophone" Puzzle (page 86). Pictured here is one possible solution to this puzzle.

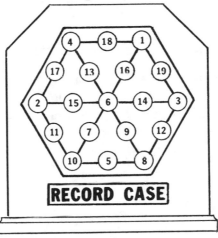

"Picture" Puzzle (page 87). The four words are:
1) *GNAT*—The bug buzzing around the minister's head.
2) *NAME*—The sign with the church's name on the tent.
3) *AMEN*—The missing word in the sermon.
4) *TENT*—The minister's tent church.

"Tattoo" Puzzle (page 88). The player must jump along the lines. One coin goes over another to a vacant circle beyond. The sequence of moves is: 3–7; 9–5; 13–3; 11–13; 1–11; 3–7; 2–12; 13–7; 4–10; 11–13; 13–7. The last coin ends up on the center circle.

"Addition" Puzzle (page 89). In the solution, two odd digits are used to make an odd number: $13 + 3 + 3 + 1 = 20$. (Note that 13 is composed of two digits.)

"Clown" Puzzles (page 90). 1) The whole numbers are 31 and 1. $31 \times 1 = 31$.

2) There are no esses in the name of the longest river in the world. The longest rivers are the Nile and the Amazon.

3) The time of day is a quarter to two.

"Collar" Puzzle (page 91). Cut the board into four pieces, as indicated in the drawing below. The larger square is formed by piecing together the two segments labelled "W" and "X." The three-by-three square is formed by piecing together segments "Y" and "Z."

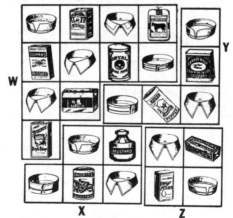

"Diner" Puzzle (page 92). "One on the city" is a glass of water. Here's one way to solve this problem:

$$
\begin{array}{r}
759 \\
75 \\
629 \\
\hline
1463
\end{array}
$$

"Puzzle Poker" Puzzle (page 93). Pictured below is one of several possible card arrangements that will solve this puzzle.

"Automobile" Puzzle (page 94). Originally he paid $15,000 for the Duesenberg and $5,000 for the Packard. He made $1,500 on the sale of the Duesenberg and he lost $500 on the sale of the Packard, for a net gain of $1,000. $1,000, five percent of the original purchase price of the two cars, was High Pockets' profit.

"Maze" Puzzle (page 95). Pictured below is the solution to Mr. Carroll's maze.

"Dancing" Puzzle (page 96). Elsie and Ambrose completed one-fifth of the marathon. If they were dancing at the rate of 3 miles per hour, they would have had 12 miles to go in a 15-mile marathon. If they increased their speed to 4 miles per hour, they would have needed only 3 hours more to complete the 12 miles, making 4 hours their total marathon time for this 15-mile dance.

"Sock Sale" Puzzle (page 97). Here's how Aunt Hattie apportioned her purchases:

Long winter socks	3 pairs @	$1.60 =	$4.80
Calf-high socks	15 pairs @	.20 =	3.00
Short socks	2 pairs @	.10 =	.20
		Total	$8.00

"Telegraphers" Puzzle (page 98). Did you tap out the following answers on your sounder?

Key #1—Impossib*le! O, pard*on me, by no means.

Key #2—The lam*b is on*e of my pets.

Key #3—At la*st a g*irl moved.

Key #4—He ma*de er*rors on purpose.

Key #5—Wel*l, I on*ly *got ter*rified out of my wits.

"Enigma" Puzzle (page 99). The first two lines of the verse refer to the word "just" while the second two lines refer to the word "ice." Put them together and they refer to the commodity that the judge so liberally dispensed in his court, namely "justice."

"Dictionary" Puzzle (page 100). The answers are as follows: 1–G; 2–Q; 3–J; 4–B; 5–E; 6–O; 7–P; 8–K; 9–C; 10–H; 11–F; 12–M.

"Key Holder" Puzzle (page 101). Loosen the central loop and pass the key through it. Next, pull the two hanging strands downwards until the loops at the back of the cardboard come through the hole to the front of the puzzle. These loops can then be put through the key. After doing that you can slide the key over so it hangs on the right loop. Pull the loops back through the hole and the puzzle is solved.

"Lunch Tray" Puzzle (page 102). "Muscles" carried 54 trays on the first trip and 45 trays on the second. Two-thirds of 54 equals 36, and 36 is four-fifths of 45. How did you stack up on this one?

About the Author

Charles Barry Townsend has been writing books dealing with puzzles, games, and magic for 25 years. He is the author of 21 books, including *The World's Most Incredible Puzzles, The World's Hardest Puzzles, The World's Greatest Puzzles, World's Greatest Magic Tricks,* and *Great Victorian Puzzle Book,* all published by Sterling Publishing Company. Mr. Townsend lives in Mill Creek, Washington, where he has recently started a puzzle newsletter on the Internet Information Highway. If you'd like to say hello, you can reach Mr. Townsend on e-mail at puzzler@ix.netcom.com.

Pictured below are the author and his dog, Jackie, checking over some of the books they've worked on together. Jackie's in charge of the doggie puzzles. You'll find her puzzle on page 49.

Index

Answer pages are in italics